Jack and The Beanstalk

Jack and the Beanstalk

Adapted and Illustrated by
D. William Johnson

Little, Brown and Company
Boston   Toronto

Books by D. William Johnson

THE WILLOW FLUTE
A North Country Tale

JACK AND THE BEANSTALK

Library of Congress Cataloging in Publication Data

Johnson, Dana William.
  Jack and the beanstalk.

  SUMMARY: A boy climbs to the top of a giant beanstalk
where he must use his quick wits to outsmart an ogre and
make his and his mother's fortune.
  [1. Fairy tales. 2. Folklore—England. 3. Giants—
Fiction] I. Jack and the beanstalk.
PZ8.J457Jac   [398.2] [E]   76-3527
ISBN 0-316-46941-6

*Published simultaneously in Canada
by Little, Brown & Company (Canada) Limited*

PRINTED IN THE UNITED STATES OF AMERICA

Dedicated to Pen, Bob, Jim, Becky, & R.

ONCE UPON A TIME there was a poor widow who lived in a little cottage with her only son Jack. Jack was a giddy, thoughtless young man, but very kindhearted and affectionate.

One year there was a hard winter, and after it the poor woman had suffered from fever and chills. Jack did no work as yet, and by degrees they grew poorer and poorer. The widow saw that there was no means of keeping Jack and herself from starvation but by selling her cow, so one morning she said to her son: "I am too weak to go myself, Jack, so you must take the cow to market for me and sell her."

Jack liked going to market to sell the cow, but as he was on his way he met a butcher who had some beautiful beans in his hand. Jack stopped to look at them. The butcher said that they were of great value, and persuaded the silly fellow to sell the cow for the beans.

When he brought them home to his mother instead of the money she expected, she was very angry, and shed many tears, scolding Jack for his mistake. He was very sorry, and they both went to bed that night thinking their last hope was gone.

☙ 9 ❧

At daybreak Jack rose and went out into the garden.

"At least," he thought, "I will sow the beans. Mother says that they are just plain scarlet-runners, and nothing else, but I may as well plant them."

So he took a piece of stick and made some holes in the ground, and put in the beans.

That day they had very little dinner, and then went sadly to bed, knowing there was nothing left to eat the next day.

Unable to sleep from hunger and grief, Jack got up at dawn and went out into the garden. He was amazed to find that the beans had grown in the night. They had climbed up and up until they reached the top of the high cliff that sheltered the cottage, and disappeared above it. The tendrils had twisted and twined themselves until they neatly formed a ladder.

"It would be easy to climb," thought Jack, and once the idea was in his head he resolved to carry it through. However, since he had foolishly traded the cow, he first decided to ask his mother's advice.

JACK CALLED his mother, and they both gazed in silent wonder at the giant beanstalk.

"I wonder where it ends," said Jack to his mother. "I would like to climb it and see."

His mother pleaded with him not to venture up the strange ladder, but Jack coaxed for her consent. He was certain he was meant to climb the wonderful beanstalk, so at last she gave in to his wishes.

Jack began to climb at once, up and up the ladderlike stalk until everything—the cottage, the village, and even the tall church spire—looked quite small.

Jack still could not see the top of the beanstalk. He felt a little tired and for a moment thought he ought to go back. But he remembered that the way to succeed in anything is never to give up, and so after resting a moment he went on.

Climbing higher and higher, until he grew afraid to look down, Jack at last reached the top of the beanstalk. He found himself in a beautiful country with fine woods and golden meadows dotted with sheep. A crystalline stream wound its way through the pastures, and not far off stood an old stone castle.

Wondering why he had never seen or heard of the castle, he saw it was separated from the village by the cliffs on which it stood, as if it were in another land.

As Jack stood looking at the castle a very strange-looking woman came out of the forest and seemed to glide toward him.

She wore a pointed cap of quilted red velvet trimmed with ermine, her hair streamed loose over her shoulders, and she carried a staff. Jack removed his cap and made a deep bow.

"Excuse me, ma'am," he said, "but is that your house?"

"No, it isn't," said the strange woman, "but listen and I shall tell you its story.

"Once upon a time there was a knight who lived in the castle, which stands at the edge of fairyland. He had a beautiful and beloved wife and several lovely children. As he was friendly to his neighbors in fairyland, the little people gave him many rare and wonderful gifts.

"Rumors of these treasures spread, and a monstrous giant who lived at no great distance, and who was a wicked being, decided to have the treasures for himself.

"So he bribed a false servant to let him into the castle when the knight was asleep, and he killed him in his bed. Then he went to the part of the castle which was the nursery and also killed the sleeping children.

"Happily for her, the lady was not to be found. She had gone with her infant son to visit her old nurse who lived in the valley; and she had been detained there all night by a storm.

"Early the next morning one of the servants who had managed to escape from the castle arrived at the old nurse's house. He told the lady the sad fate of her husband and children. At first she was anxious to return to the castle and share in the misfortune of her family. But the old nurse, amid many tears, begged her to remain for the sake of her infant son.

"At last the lady consented to stay in hiding at the nurse's home, for the servant said that the giant meant to murder her and the baby if ever he found them.

"Years rolled on. The old nurse died, leaving her cottage and what little she owned to the poor lady, who continued to live there, working as a peasant does for her daily bread. There was a pleasant little garden behind the cowshed, where they grew vegetables, and with that, a spinning wheel, and the milk from the cow, they managed to stay alive.

"Jack, that poor lady is your mother. The castle was once your father's, and must again be yours."

Jack uttered a cry of surprise.

"My mother! Oh, what ought I to do? My lost father! My dear mother!"

"Your duty requires you to win it back for your mother. But the task is a very difficult one, and full of danger, Jack. Have you the courage to undertake it?"

"If I am doing right I should fear nothing," answered Jack.

"Then," said the lady in the red cap, "you are one of those who slays giants. You must get into the castle and, if possible, take back the hen that lays the golden eggs and the harp that talks. Remember, all that the giant possesses is really yours." And as she stopped speaking she disappeared. Jack knew, of course, that she was a fairy.

Determined to begin immediately, Jack walked to the castle and blew the horn which hung beside the door. The portal opened and a frightful giantess with one great eye in the middle of her forehead appeared.

As soon as Jack saw her he turned to run away, but she caught him and dragged him into the castle.

"Ho, ho!" she laughed terribly. "I can see you didn't expect to find *me* here. No, I won't let you go again. I am weary of my life. I am so overworked. I don't see why I oughtn't have a servant like other ladies. So you shall be my boy. You shall clean the knives and black the boots, and make the fires and help me when the giant is out. When he is home I shall hide you, for he has eaten up all my other boys, and you would be a dainty morsel indeed!"

She dragged Jack into the kitchen while she spoke, and although he was frightened, he struggled to be brave and make the best of things.

"I am willing to help you and do all I can to make your work easier," he said, "but I beg you to hide me well, for I should not like to be eaten."

"That's a good fellow," said the giantess, nodding her head. "You're lucky that you didn't scream or cry out when you saw me, as the others have, or you would have wakened my husband and that would have been the end of you! Come here. Go into my wardrobe. He never ventures to open that. You will be safe there."

She opened a huge wardrobe which stood in the great hall, and shut him into it. The keyhole was so large that he had plenty of air, and he could see everything that took place through it. By and by he heard a heavy tramping on the stairs like the roaring of cannons,

and then a voice like thunder cried out:

> "*Fe, fi, fo-fum,*
> *I smell the blood of an Englishman.*
> *Be he live or be he dead,*
> *I'll grind his bones to make my bread.*"

"Wife," cried the giant, "I smell a man in the castle. Serve him to me for breakfast!"

"I think you must be growing old and stupid," replied the giantess in loud tones. "It isn't a man you smell, but a nice fresh elephant steak I have cooked you for breakfast. Now sit down and eat."

She placed a huge dish of the savory meat before him and he was so greatly pleased that he forgot all about the idea of an Englishman being in the castle. After breakfast he went out for a walk; and then the giantess opened the wardrobe and made Jack come out to help her. He worked all day, she fed him well, and when evening came she put Jack back into the wardrobe.

THE GIANT came in to supper and Jack watched through the keyhole. He was amazed to see the giant pick clean an ox's bone and put a whole roasted chicken into his mouth at one time.

When supper was done he ordered his wife to bring him his hen that laid the golden eggs.

The giantess went away, and soon returned with a large white hen, which she placed on the table before her husband. "And now, my dear," she said, "I am going for a walk if you need me no longer."

"Go," said the giant, "I shall be happy to have a nap by and by."

Then he took up the white hen and said to her:

"Lay!" And instantly she laid a golden egg.

"Lay!" said the giant again, and she laid another.

"Lay!" he repeated a third time. And again a golden egg was laid on the table.

Now Jack was sure that this was the hen of which the fairy had spoken.

Shortly afterward the giant put the hen on the floor and then fell

fast asleep, snoring so loudly it sounded as if an earthquake were shaking the castle.

Seeing the giant was asleep, Jack pushed open the wardrobe door and crept out. Stealing across the room, he picked up the hen and made his way to the kitchen door, which stood ajar. He opened it, shut it and locked it behind him. Then running to the beanstalk, he descended as quickly as he was able.

When his mother saw him enter the house she wept for joy, for she feared the fairies had carried him off, or that the giant had captured him. But Jack put down the hen before her, telling her how he had been in the giant's castle and of all his adventures. She was very glad to see the hen, which would make them rich once more.

NE DAY when his mother had gone to market Jack made another journey up the beanstalk, but first he dyed his hair and stained his face with walnut juice. The giantess didn't recognize him, dragging him in as she had done before to help with the work. But she heard her husband coming and hid him in the wardrobe, not guessing it was the same man who had stolen the hen. She told him to be still or the giant would eat him, and busied herself in the kitchen.

Then the giant came in saying:

> *"Fe, fi, fo-fum,*
> *I smell the blood of an Englishman.*
> *Be he live or be he dead,*
> *I'll grind his bones to make my bread."*

"Nonsense!" said his wife. "It is only the roasted pig that I thought would be a nice tidbit for your supper. Sit down and I shall bring it to you at once." The giant sat down, soon his wife brought the roasted pig on a huge platter, and they began their supper. Jack was amazed to see them pick the bones of the pig as clean as if it had been a sparrow.

As soon as they had finished their meal the giantess rose and said loudly:

"Now, my dear, with your permission I am going up to my room to finish the story I am reading. Call if you want me."

"First," answered the giant, "bring me my money bags that I may count my golden pieces before I sleep." The giantess obeyed. She went and soon returned with two leather bags over her shoulder, which she put down by her husband.

"There," she said, "that is all that's left of the knight's money. When you have spent it all you will have to rob a baron."

"That," thought Jack, "he will never do if only I can prevent it."

When his wife was gone the giant took out heaps and heaps of golden pieces, counted them and put them in piles. When he tired of

this amusement he swept them all back into the bags, leaned back in his chair and fell asleep. His snoring was so loud that nothing else could be heard.

Jack stole softly from the wardrobe and took up the bags of money that once were his father's. He ran off with great difficulty, descended the beanstalk, and laid the bags of gold on his mother's table. She had just returned from town and was crying when Jack was nowhere to be found.

"There, Mother, I have returned my father's gold."

"Oh, Jack! You are a very brave boy, but I wish you wouldn't risk your precious neck in the giant's castle. Tell me how you came to go there again."

And Jack told her all about it.

FTER A TIME Jack made up his mind to go again to the giant's castle, so he climbed the beanstalk once more and blew the horn at the giant's door. The giantess opened the door. She was a stupid creature and didn't recognize him. Fearing another robbery, she stopped before taking him in, but Jack's face was so innocent that she couldn't resist him. So she took him in again and hid him in the wardrobe.

Shortly afterward the giant came home, and as soon as he had crossed the threshold he roared out:

> "Fe, fi, fo-fum,
> I smell the blood of an Englishman.
> Be he live or be he dead,
> I'll grind his bones to make my bread."

"You stupid old giant," said his wife, "you only smell a nice fat sheep, which I have grilled for your dinner."

And the giant sat down while his wife brought a whole sheep and a tub of cooked apples for his dinner. When he had eaten it all up he said:

"Now bring me my harp, and I will have a little music while you take your walk."

The giantess obeyed and returned with a beautiful harp. The framework was sparkling with diamonds and rubies, and the strings were made of gold.

He drew the harp toward him and said:

"Play!"

And the harp, his faithful servant, played a very soft, sad song.

"Play something merrier!" said the giant.

And the harp played a merry song.

"Now play me a lullaby," roared the giant, and the harp played a sweet lullaby, which put the giant to sleep.

Then Jack crept out of the wardrobe and went into the kitchen to see if the giantess was out. Finding no one there he quietly opened the door, for he thought it would be difficult to escape with the harp in his hands.

Then he entered the giant's room and seized the harp and ran away with it. But as he jumped over the threshold the harp called:

"Master! Master!"

And the giant woke up.

With a tremendous roar he sprang from his chair and reached the door in two strides.

Jack fled like lightning with the harp, talking to it as he went. He told it he was the son of its old master, the knight.

The giant ran so quickly that he was soon quite near to Jack. But as he stretched out his great hand to catch him he stepped on a loose stone and fell to the ground.

This accident gave Jack enough time to get on the beanstalk and hurry downward, but as he reached the bottom he saw the giant descending after him.

"Mother! Mother!" cried Jack, "fetch me the axe as quickly as you can."

His mother ran to him with a hatchet in her hand and with one strong blow Jack cut nearly through the beanstalk.

"Now, Mother, stand out of the way," he said.

J ACK'S MOTHER shrank back, and it was well she did, for just as the giant took hold of the last branch of the beanstalk Jack cut it through and darted from the spot.

The beanstalk tottered and fell, and down came the giant with a terrible crash, breaking his neck, lying dead at the feet of Jack and his mother.

Before the two recovered from the shock a beautiful lady appeared before them.

"Jack," she said, "you have acted like a brave knight's son, and you deserve to have your inheritance restored to you. Dig a grave and bury the giant."

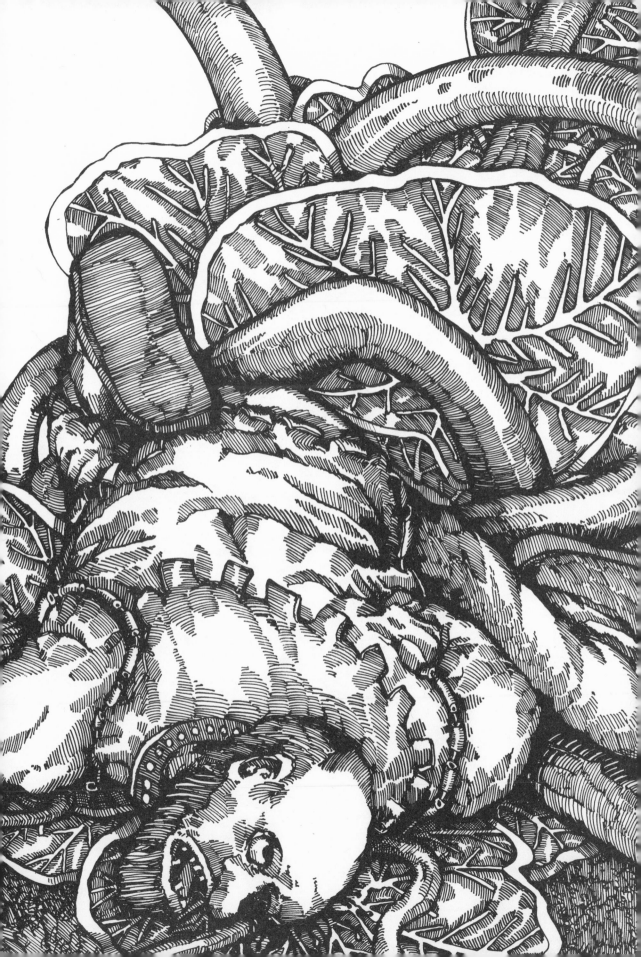

When the giant was buried she said:

"Now you must go and kill the giantess."

"But," said Jack, "I could not kill anybody unless I was fighting with him, and I cannot draw my sword upon a woman. Moreover, the giantess was very kind to me."

The fairy smiled at Jack.

"I am pleased with your generous feelings," she said. "Neverthe-

less, return to the castle and act as you know in your heart you must."

Jack asked the fairy if she would show him the way to the castle, as the beanstalk was now down. She told him she would drive him there in her chariot, which was drawn by a flying horse. Jack thanked her and sat down in the chariot.

The fairy drove a long distance until they reached a village nestled at the foot of the hill.

There they found many poor peasants assembled and the fairy stopped to address them.

"My friends," she said, "the cruel giant who oppressed you for so long, who ate your herds and flocks, is dead. This young man has freed you from him forever. He is the son of your kind old master, the knight."

At this the men gave a loud cheer and told Jack they would serve him as faithfully as they had his father. So the fairy bade them to follow her to the castle, and off they marched, Jack leading the troop.

Jack blew the horn when they reached the castle, but the giantess saw them coming from a lookout slit in the turret. She was very frightened, for she guessed something had happened to her husband, and as she came downstairs she caught her foot in the hem of her dress and fell from the top to the bottom, breaking *her* neck.

When the people outside found the door locked they broke it down and stormed inside. Nobody was to be seen, but on leaving the hall they found the body of the giantess at the foot of the stairs.

So Jack took possession of the castle. The fairy went and brought his mother to him with the money, the hen and the harp.

Before her departure for fairyland, the fairy explained to Jack that she had sent the butcher to meet him with the beans, in order to see what sort of fellow he was.

"If you had looked up at the gigantic beanstalk and only stupidly wondered about it," she said, "I should have left you where your misfortune placed you, only restoring the cow to your mother. But you showed an inquiring mind, great courage, and enterprise, therefore you deserve to rise. When you mounted the beanstalk, Jack, you climbed the ladder of fortune."

And then she disappeared.

So Jack showed his mother the harp. They sold the golden eggs and became very rich again. Jack married a beautiful princess, and they all lived happily ever after.